'Edna O'Brien might be the ultimate Joyce's woman: she has used him as a lodestar throughout her literary career, neither daunted by his dominance nor intimidated by his bawdiness . . . [The play] provides a singular biographical view of James Joyce, his literary achievements juggled alongside the intensity of his real life. And while Joyce may have loved all these women represented on the stage, the primary love affair here is between Edna O'Brien herself and the ghost of a literary hero.' *Irish Independent*

'Offers its heroines visceral freedom . . . [Scenes] brim with strange, effervescent energy that channels the modernist spirit of Joyce's writing.' *Financial Times*

'O'Brien's dreamlike, reflective play brings Joycean language to life . . . *Joyce's Women* dismisses present-day debate about separating art from the artist . . . [Instead, it] explores the process of "transmuting the daily bread of experience into the radiant body of everliving life" in all its complexity.' *New York Times*

'Admirably ambitious . . . offers breathtaking moments of vision and a bracing refusal to pin people to certainties.' *Observer*

'There's no cancelling of James Joyce here . . . O'Brien has never been a puritan. Hers is a big, forgiving, human soul. Though her writing is often vivid, she's always seen the world in shades of grey.' *Irish Examiner*

T0333843

Joyce's Women

Edna O'Brien is the recipient of many awards, including the Irish PEN Lifetime Achievement Award, the American National Arts Gold Medal, the Frank O'Connor Prize, the PEN/Nabokov Award for Achievement in International Literature, and the David Cohen Prize for Literature. In 2021, she was appointed Commandeur of French Arts and Letters. Born and raised in the west of Ireland, Edna O'Brien has lived in London for many years.

EDNA O'BRIEN

Joyce's Women

faber

First published in 2022
by Faber and Faber Limited
74–77 Great Russell Street
London WC1B 3DA

This edition published in 2023

Typeset by Brighton Gray
Printed and bound in the UK by CPI Group (Ltd), Croydon CR0 4YY

A CIP record for this book
is available from the British Library

978–0–571–38604–8

2 4 6 8 10 9 7 5 3 1

Joyce's Women was first performed at the Abbey Theatre, Dublin, in a co-production between the Abbey Theatre and Eilene Davidson Productions, on 17 September 2022. The cast, in order of appearance, was as follows:

Zozimus Bill Murphy
May Joyce Deirdre Donnelly
Nora Barnacle Bríd Ní Neachtain
Brigitte Zimmerman Hilda Fay
Lucia Joyce Genevieve Hulme Beaman
Martha Fleischmann Caitríona Ní Mhurchú
Harriet Shaw Weaver Ali White
Stanislaus Joyce Patrick Moy
James Joyce Stephen Hogan
Young Boy/Waiter Emmet Farrell

Director Conall Morrison
Set Design Sabine Dargent
Costume Design Joan O'Clery
Lighting Design Ben Ormerod
Composer Conor Linehan
Sound Design Ivan Birthistle
Movement Director Justine Doswell
Producer Craig Flaherty
Casting Director Sarah Jones
Voice Director Andrea Ainsworth

Characters

James Joyce

Stanislaus Joyce
younger brother of Joyce

May Joyce
mother of Joyce; a ghost

Nora Barnacle
wife of Joyce

Brigitte Zimmermann
seamstress in Zurich

Lucia Joyce
daughter of James and Nora

Martha Fleischmann
briefly inamorata of Joyce

Harriet Shaw Weaver
patron of Joyce

Zozimus
blind balladeer

Young Boy

Waiter, Prostitutes, Nurse, Justine, Voices

JOYCE'S WOMEN

SCENE ONE

Paris, 1900s.
'Tim Finnegan' ballad sung by Zozimus in darkness.

Zozimus (*singing*)
   'Whack folte dah, dance to your partners
   Welt the flure your trotters shake,
   Wasn't it the truth I told you,
   Lots of fun at Finnegan's wake.'

Lights come up.
   *Downstage a table covered in a simple white cloth
   with a vase of red roses.*
   A heavy, hexagonal glass bottle of ink.
   *A curtain separates the front from the body of the
   stage.*
   *Six women are onstage in front of the table. They are
   of different ages and their dress indicates something of
   their circumstances. They are:*
   May Joyce (ghost – mother of James Joyce).
   Nora Barnacle (his wife).
   Brigitte Zimmermann (seamstress in Zurich).
   Lucia Joyce (daughter of James and Nora).
   Martha Fleischmann (briefly inamorata of Joyce).
   Harriet Shaw Weaver (Miss Weaver, patron of Joyce).
   *On a windowsill to the left of the group is an old man,
   partially blind, playing softly on a mouth organ. This is
   Zozimus, whose singing threads the play.*

'The harlot's cry from street to street
Shall weave old Ireland's winding-sheet.
The winner's shout, the loser's curse,
Dance before dead Ireland's hearse.'

3

The women go offstage.

From the opposite side, Stanislaus Joyce, younger brother of James, walks on in an old pullover and soft hat.

Stanislaus In the nursery long ago, when times were good and we had a piano, Jim wrote playlets which he put to music, to entertain the younger children. His favourite story was Adam and Eve from the Bible. Our little Eva played Eve, and Charlie played Adam. Jim played the Devil.

As Stanislaus goes, James Joyce – in his thirties, pale linen jacket, tennis shoes and straw hat – enters. He is carrying an ash plant.

A French female singer is heard offstage.

Joyce is muttering the words of Finnegans Wake and continues as he sits at the table with his little notebook and starts to write.

A waiter plonks a glass of wine in front of him.

Joyce speaks the words aloud as he writes them with pen and ink. We hear his Dublin accent at the moments when he speaks louder.

Joyce . . . All the birds of the sea,
they trolled out right bold when
they smacked the big kuss of Tristan and Isolde . . .
sea-words wind-words in the waves length . . .

Into his writing reverie, the voices of saucy Dublin prostitutes intrude.

Joyce goes on writing but the voices of the prostitutes grow stronger and more jocular.

Girl 1 Tatters and kippers
I'd sooner his knickers.

Girl 2 (*sympathetic*) I'm Bertha Supple . . . on your lonesome are you?

Girl 3 He's bashful . . . His cock's adrone.

4

Girl 2 He's writin' a buke.

Girl 1 Have a gawk.

Girl 2 (*quoting from a page that has slipped out of Joyce's notebook*) 'Would one were to do apart a lilybit her virginelles . . .'

Girl 1 Cripes.

Girl 2 Maybe he's a medico.

Girl 4 How's his wick, Nell?

Nell Usual . . . Kineshite quiver.

Girl 4 Give him a Birdie.

> *They all hoot with laughter.*
> *Joyce turns aside as if he can evade them, which he cannot.*

Meek-Voiced Girl Mister, sir . . . Me granny's dying with the croup.

Girls (*shouting her down*) Oh there goes Miss Meek.
She keeps a house of imprudence.
She has a big black parlour
For poxy old medical students.

> *They laugh as they recite.*

All Together He gave it to Nelly
To stick in her belly
The leg o' the duck
The leg o' the duck
For he was a jolly old medico

> *They all repeat the rhyme in song as Joyce gestures frantically for them to shut up and go away.*

Girl 4 I'm Zoe . . . I'm luscious . . . Ho ho ho . . . Threepence a go . . . Sixpence for doggy . . . Ten bob for a full night . . .

Meek-Voiced Girl Mister . . . Give me a penny to light a candle in the Pro Cathedral . . . She'll go straight to heaven . . . and so will you.

Joyce empties the loose change from his pocket which rolls all over the floor.

Joyce Be gone . . . I am finished with all of you.

Joyce stands and hits the table several times with his stick and the voices and chatter gradually fade.
  The ghost of May Joyce enters in brown sackcloth, ashes on her mouth, her voice plaintive and rapid.
  Joyce does not acknowledge her arrival.

May My sunny Jim . . . My chosen boy.
  When your father sent you to Clongowes Wood, to the Jesuits, at six and a half, our house was a wake.
  You looked so smart in your Little Lord Fauntleroy's outfit.
  You clung to me. Your father and my father fought in the car.
  That cheeky snib Eileen Vance from number seven stood outside our kitchen window, serenading you.

Zozimus (*singing the Eileen Vance song*)
  'Oh Jimmy Joyce, you are my darlin',
  You are my looking glass, night and mornin'
  I'd rather have you without a farthin'
  Than Jimmy Jakes with his ass and garden . . .'

May The weekly letter home!
  Older boys ragging you about missing me,
  missing the rice I boiled specially for you.
  My kisses and the Holy Host on your tongue were the two things you revered most. Before they made you an Altar Boy you wrote a hymn to the two mothers: the Virgin Mary and me.
  As a young child you kept vigil over the dead infants who had died down the years. It marked you. Envisaging

death creeping from their extremities, right up to the glowing centres of their brains.

It was after we had to take you out of Clongowes, for lack of funds, that you changed . . . and not for the better.

Since he does not acknowledge her, she moves closer to him and prods him hard with his stick.

(*Sharply.*) Have you no word to throw at me?

Joyce ignores her and goes on writing.

(*More urgent.*) Me having to hold everything together – tea, fried bread and dripping . . .Your father grinding his teeth and your sister Poppy begging him the day he got his meagre pension to bring some home. And I knew you were becoming lost to us. I heard from a priest that you associated with prostitutes, but I was too cowed by then to tackle you. Paris was your goal. To be continentalised. Paris – the Yvonnes and the Madeleines, the tumbled beauties, their mouths yellowed with the pus of flan bretons. When I was packing for you to go, I said I hoped that away from home you might learn what the heart is and what it feels. HAVE YOU?

Joyce ignores the question and reads aloud from a loose page.

Joyce (*reading*) I go forth to forge in the smithy of my soul, the uncreated conscience of my race.

May (*sarcastic*) Am I not your race . . .

I wrote to you constantly, with enclosures, telling you to be careful, not to drink the tap water unless it was filtered. I did not mention the Yvonnes and the Madeleines. Had to sell our good carpet to send money to you, and you rebuked me for sending the postal order on a Saturday, because it meant you had to go hungry for thirty-six hours, or so you said. I wasn't as stupid as you thought, Jim. Selling and pawning things to keep you in style. Requests every day to me or to Stan, to return a library book or to borrow another one. The buttons on your good trousers had come off, so I must acquire more. You requested a hat, a blue felt hat. You must have thought I'd won the sweep. Your literary cronies in Dublin informing everyone of your nocturnes, and of course it got back to me. It was not vespers at Notre Dame as you pretended. Never crossed your mind that I was dying. Worn out from childbearing and your father's rages. You came in answer to the telegram – *Mother dying, Come home.* Little Babbie beside my bed and me, raving, seeing buttercups on the white quilt and she saw them too.

Joyce (*coldly*) When I looked at you there, pale, dead, I cursed the system that caused it – our doomed race and the stranglehold of the Catholic Church.

May Yet you would not kneel, when my brother begged you to do your Easter Duty. You would not grant a dying mother's wish.

Joyce I would not submit . . .

May (*interrupting*) Aye. The pride of intellect. The curse of Lucifer and his cohorts, banished to Hell. Forever . . . Ever. O dire word. O dire fate. Vault after vault of hellfire. Fire that gives scalding heat but no light. Hell is darkness, endless darkness. Fallen angels, demons stoking those fires and hating and cursing the newly arrived. Think. Think what you are losing, and for what . . . Earthly temptation. The desires of the flesh. Never to see the light of God or his angels again.

Joyce I am not afraid to make a mistake, even a great mistake, a lifelong mistake. And perhaps as long as eternity too.

May With your haunted ink pots – (*She picks it up violently.*) and your command of the Word you have consigned yourself to Hell.

Joyce (*interrupting suddenly*) Cancer killed you . . . not I.

8

May A gypsy called to our house one day for a sup of milk and she drank it and then looked at you and saw by your steel-blue eyes that there were two things that would forever haunt you – you would lose your mind and die a pauper.

(*Up close to him.*) Never send to know for whom the bell tolls . . . It tolls for thee.

I will haunt you to the end.

May goes.

Joyce looks after her thoughtfully, as he screws the top back on the ink bottle.

He recalls a line he once wrote about her, and recites it with detachment.

Joyce A gaud of amber beads in a linen kerchief . . .

Darkness.
End of scene.

SCENE TWO

Brigitte's Gasthaus. January 1941.
Very early morning.
Dim light from a corridor.

A woman in her fifties wearing a long, dark coat and cloche hat enters from the street. She removes the coat but keeps the hat on. It is clear that she is weary. She goes to the table and sits and sighs. From her cardigan pocket, she takes a handkerchief with four or five of Joyce's rings. She looks at them and kisses one.

It is a large-ish kitchen, somewhat untidy, stove already lit.

Brigitte, a seamstress, has given shelter to James and Nora Joyce since they arrived, penniless, from France.

One of the main features is Brigitte's foot machine. Strewn around are various garments on chairs and wooden clothes horses.

9

There are also her other sewing needs, thimbles, pins, pincushions, measuring tapes, spools of thread, bales of cloth, and several pairs of scissors, including a large steel tailor's scissors.

The long wooden table has been moved in and is bare, except at the far end is a tall pewter candlestick with one candle wedged in it and a taper nearby.

On the table is a white Holy Communion dress, and in the dim light, it resembles a little corpse.

Brigitte, the owner of the Gasthaus, appears from a corridor to the left of the stage, and jumps when she sees Nora. She turns on a stronger light.

Brigitte (*softly*) How is Herr Joyce?

Nora It was a five-hour operation . . . he had a duodenal ulcer in his stomach that was there for many years.

My poor Jim.

Brigitte Nora, he has come through.

Nora He always dreaded death.

As a young child, he would keep watch over the infants in their family that had died. And he would imagine the bright centres of their brains

being extinguished one by one,

like street lamps . . .

What is he dreaming now . . .

Brigitte They say you never dream anything during anaesthetic.

Everything is wiped out. *Vergessene.*

Nora I asked if a bed could be put next to his, so as I could be there next to him.

They refused. (*She holds up the collection of rings.*)

These are his.

He believes in signs, numbers, wizardry and all sorts of Irish piseogs . . . Cracked mad.

Brigitte (*looking at the rings*) Will I put them somewhere safe. (*As she does it.*) Which of Herr Joyce's books is your favourite?

Nora Couldn't read any of them. Too highfalutin . . . He'd have made a better living as a concert singer . . . he had the most beautiful tenor voice . . .

Brigitte walks back and touches Nora by the shoulders.

Brigitte (*leading her to the stove*) You're perished . . . Come to the stove and let this be your personal armchair.

Silence.
    Nora hesitates for a few seconds, then rallies, and regains some cheer because of Brigitte's kindness. Her next speech is rapid, excited and in a Connaught brogue.

Nora Sauntered into my life he did . . . I was looking at gorgeous furs in Barnado's window. I took him for a Norseman with his sailor's cap and his sea-blue eyes . . . We started going out . . . I couldn't follow what he was saying – 'Proteus, God of the Sea . . .'
    . . . The deep breast of the waves . . . the seaweed, black, emerald and olive under the current . . . I was used to lads that herded sheep and had clean white shirts of a Sunday.
    Couldn't think what he saw in me, but he did. Swept me off my feet . . . I was his wild flower of the rain-drenched hedges, made beautiful by moonlight, his soul trembling beside mine . . . I was the other half of Ireland,
    that he wanted for his writing . . . Every single little secret, he wheedled out of me. Even the colour of my garters . . . The miraculous medal I wore, the divilment me and Mary O'Halloran got up to.
    Out in the fields in the sun, half naked, standing on dung hills with heads of cabbage,
    trying to guess the initials of the men we would marry.
    Before long . . . we are going out steady. Letters pouring in to Finn's hotel where I worked as a chambermaid . . .

I read them in the lavatory and hid them in a copy book –
how he hated God and Death, how he liked Nora.

Sleeping with a glove of mine under his pillow . . .

'Twas a Sunday and I arranged a picnic . . . stuff pinched
from the hotel.

Pan bread, cooked ham, pickles and slices of seed cake.

We'd climbed to Howth Head . . . Scorching day, place
all to ourselves.

Wild geese and gannets honking and malarking up in the
high heavens . . .

He mustn't have eaten for a week, finally I fed him the
last bit of seedcake from my mouth . . . The mother bird
feeding her young.

We lay back in the cool of the beds of fern . . . O wonder.
His eyes fixed upon me, when a fella, a sort of tramp came
up the hill, and he said 'caught you . . . caught you . . .' and
went off cursing and blinding. It was a trap.

Next morning manager of the hotel calls me in . . . big
stout Mayo woman . . . said she had no choice but to
inform my parents and soon the anonymous letter.

Jim was an infidel at war with Mother Church and
Mother Ireland.

He went with Women of the Night over by Mabbot
Street.

I wrote him a goodbye.

Brigitte Oh no!

Nora I hinted about a boy back home, who had courted.

*The scene is interrupted by three short whistles and the
word 'Noretta. Noretta.'*

Jesus . . . It's him . . . It's Jim.

Flashback.
Nora jumps up and down, throws off her heavy cardigan and runs helter-skelter, pins falling out of her hair and she looks more youthful.
An operatic scene.
She arrives downstage where Joyce, in ragged clothes under the eave of the window, is still dripping from rain with a sheet of newspaper over his head.

Nora (*defiant*) You're a mad man.

Joyce Why do you torture me?

Nora All I said was a name.

Joyce A name! Michael Bodkin. A sweetheart's name.

Nora Yes, a sweetheart's name.

Joyce (*angry*) I have to meet him.

Nora You can't. He's dead.

Pause.

He died for love of me. When he heard I was leaving for Dublin he got out of his sickbed to sing beneath my window.

Joyce What song did he sing?

Nora I'm not telling you.

Joyce (*moves much nearer, getting frantic*) I have to know everything about you. There is nothing you can conceal . . .
What colour hair had he?

Nora Black. Jet-black like the Spanish Conquistadores.

Joyce Where is he buried?

Nora Why?

Joyce I want to go there.

Nora You can't.

Joyce Where?

Nora Oughterard . . . Fifteen Irish miles out of Galway. (*Emphatic.*) You don't own me.

Joyce (*exclaiming*) What song did he sing?

Nora I won't tell you.

Joyce (*pleading*) Noretta my sea bird, my soar bird, my barnacle bird, come away with me.
I am a pilgrim on life's crooked path . . . Be my life's companion.

Nora Be your life's companion!
I hear from your cronies you are trying to get a lute and go to England and play old songs all the way from Falmouth up to Margate.

Joyce I tried to break with you and kill every image of you, including your glove under my pillow, but I failed, I failed, you kept pulling me back, back.
Life is waiting for us.

Nora You have never once said the word love.

Joyce I honour you so much . . . no one understands me as you do . . . You ask why I don't say love, but surely you must believe I am very fond of you and if to desire to possess a person wholly, to admire and honour deeply and to seek and secure that person's happiness in every way, is love, then perhaps my affection for you is love.

Nora Oh brave words.

Joyce (*quickly*) I see in you an extraordinary melancholy . . .
No human being has ever stood so close to my heart as you do now . . .
I am not a comrade in lust.

From his pocket he takes a torn, short piece of paper and hands it to her.

Read this.

Nora What is it?

Joyce It is the first thing I had written in months. Read it.

Nora reads four lines of the poem.

Nora (*reading aloud*)
'In the dark pine-wood
I would we lay,
In deep cool shadow
At noon of day.

How sweet to lie there,
Sweet to kiss,
Where the great pine-forest
Enaisled is!

She begins to falter.

Thy kiss descending
Sweeter were
With a soft tumult
Of thy hair.

Here her voice grows fainter.

O unto the pine-wood
At noon of day
Come with me now,
Sweet love, away.'

She can't finish the poem without emotion.

Joyce I have offers of posts in Berlitz schools all over Europe – Paris, Berlin, Zurich, London . . .

Nora (*cutting in*) How?

Joyce I have a university degree.

Nora I can't go. I belong here.

Joyce You don't.

Nora Terrible murders happen over there, women drowned in prussic acid and dismembered . . .
My mother would have to put advertisements in every single newspaper . . . She'd have a heart attack . . .
(*Whispering.*) I can't.

Nora turns and walks in the direction from which she came.
Joyce stands watching her.

Joyce Your soul seems to me the most beautiful and melancholy soul in the world.

She melts.

Nora You break hearts, you do.

Joyce exits.

Zozimus (*singing*)
'Oh the violets are scenting the leaves, Nora,
Displaying their charms to the bees
When I first said I loved only you, Nora,
And you said you loved only me.

The chestnut blooms gleamed through the glade, Nora
A robin sang loud from a tree
When I first said I first loved only you, Nora,
And you said you loved only me.'

Nora re-enters the kitchen, where Brigitte has been watching, entranced, the scene between Nora and Joyce but not the letter to Starkey.

Brigitte So romantic!

Nora Yes!
    No post in London, none in Paris . . . he had to touch a Dublin fella to get the fare to Zurich and none there either. They had misled him. A Professor took pity on us and paid for us for one night in a Gasthaus Hoffnung.

Brigitte It means HOPE.

Nora Jim sends a telegraph to his brother Stanislaus . . .
    '*Finalement . . . Elle n'est pas encore vierge, elle est touchée.*'
    I made him translate it . . . She is not a virgin anymore . . . she has been touched.

    Brigitte turns away, a little embarrassed, and picks up the second Holy Communion dress.

We ended up in a naval town called Pola. When I lugged our battered suitcase down that gangplank, I knew I would never go home. I would never hear the whoosh of the Corrib or watch the salmon leap to get back to where they were spawned.

Brigitte I better get along as these Fräuleins are preparing to make their first Holy Communion.
    They have been practising receiving the Host by placing blobs of snow on their tongues . . .
    You have children?

Nora (*terse*) I have a son.
    He is in New York studying to be a tenor.
    He has his father's voice.

Brigitte I wish I had children.

Nora You never married?

Brigitte (*trying not to be emotional*) I was engaged.

Pause.

My wedding dress is still upstairs . . . on its hanger.

Brigitte exits with the two dresses.
    Nora sits on the chair, upset, because she has lied.
    As though it is a ghost, or perhaps a hallucination, a
figure appears.
    This is Stanislaus, in his forties, dressed completely in
black – black hat, black leather gloves and black
galoshes.
    He confronts her with a written note.

Stanislaus 'She cares nothing for my art' – Jim's very own
words.

Nora shrinks from him in dismay.
    Stanislaus assaults her with a long and cruel
monologue, laughing throughout.

So! His portable Ireland, it didn't work after all.
    You moped.
    You were not someone who could easily be transplanted.
    'Sad heart of Ruth, when sick for home she stood in tears
amid the alien corn.'
    You couldn't master any one of the four languages spoken.
    Your tirades were ungrammatical.
    He was missing his family, missing Dublin.
    Begging me, his brothers' keeper, to come.
    He needed someone he could talk to.
    He said, Stanislaus, the repressed forces of Ireland are
holding you back. You will fall foul to the prevailing
intellectual paralysis.
    True to his word he was waiting on the platform,
    a figure of fatigue.

We went to the Osteria.

He drank absinthe.

He shed tears.

He was planning to leave you.

I shall never forget my arrival in that ramshackle ménage . . .

Pots and pans all over the floor, chairs stacked on top of one another, broken crockery, Giorgio spurting water from a pistol and little Lucia sitting on the floor combing her hair for nits, which she called eggs.

What struck me most was your composure . . . your basilisk look. Not a word of welcome, except to say 'Are people in Dublin axing after me?'

Jim who had wept earlier was now singing Puccini arias and stirring noodles in a pot on the stove.

His face was scarlet.

The little girl climbed onto his shoulders and searched his head for letters of the alphabet.

He drank liberally, sometimes maggoty drunk.

You knew he did.

You knew he went with his friend Budgen to Piazza Cavona,

The celebrated brothel only a few doors away.

It had for him a talismanic name – 'The Golden Key'.

The favourite whores were Balkan.

You never challenged him.

You chose not to . . .

It was hardly clemency.

He walks around her humming now.

'Oh 'tis far and it is far

From Connemara where you are . . .'

Singing and humming that cursed song that drove him wild with jealousy.

The black-haired youths who loved you so.

For days, nay weeks, you did not speak until you had broken him down.

The penitent son begging to be taken back, back to the dark sanctuary of your womb. Save me . . . soothe me . . . succour me to your breast.

You were the Belladonna, the deadly night shade
who opens her perfumes to the night.
The soft cadence of your brogue,
a flutter of garments,
and the merry jingling of the quoits on the brass bed.
Circe had nothing on you.
Mornings again and the old tirades . . .
Jim writing on a suitcase . . .
Planetary music and chaos.

He moves close up to her face.

You took him from us.
Because you had broken from your own family,
you made sure he broke with us.
Well it's not long now.
The bright centres of that brain being extinguished . . .

He takes something bulky from his pocket: it might be a gun.

He will lay siege to literature no more . . .
The hacks are wetting their quills.

What he is holding is a large torch, which he turns on and shines mercilessly on her face. We see her flinch as she tries to back away but cannot.

Altrahora . . . the blackest hour . . . Adios, Miss Barnacle . . .

He exits.
    For the first time Zozimus engages directly with Nora, who is sitting up, terrified. He walks towards her, already singing.

Zozimus (*singing*)
    'Oh! My boat can safely float in the teeth of the wind and the weather

And outrace the fastest hooker between Galway and
Kinsale.
When the black floor of the ocean and the white foam
rush together,
High she rides, in her pride, like a sea-gull through the
gale.
(*Even more rousing.*) Oh she's neat! Oh she's sweet! She's
a beauty in ev'ry line!
The Queen of Connemara is that bounding barque of
mine.
When she's loaded down with fish till the water lips the
gunwale
Not a drop she'll take on board her that would wash a
fly away!
Oh she's neat! Oh she's sweet! She's a beauty in ev'ry
line! . . .'

SCENE FIVE

Noises of Brigitte returning.
Zozimus goes back to his seat at the windowsill.
Brigitte enters.
Nora is sitting rigid.

Brigitte Why do you tremble?

Nora (*ignoring the question*) Will we hear the telephone
from the hall?

Brigitte I'll move it in.

*Brigitte moves the telephone on a long lead and puts it
on a side table, easy to access.*

Nora I lied to you . . .
I have a daughter. He idolised her.

*Second flashback scene. Paris 1930. Nora and Brigitte
watch.*

*A girl's bedroom, cluttered – various garments, ballet
shoes hanging, a fur coat, chiffon scarves.*

*Lucia, in her twenties, is slumped in a low armchair
holding a silver-backed mirror in her hand and studying
her image carefully.*

*She does not like what she sees. She sticks her tongue
out, makes faces, is obviously in a bad mood.*

*Joyce enters from left stage wearing a torn high-necked
pullover and thick dark glasses. He watches her before
speaking.*

Joyce Want to come for a walk in the *bois*?

Lucia does not answer.

Sun is out . . . Sycamores in bloom.

Lucia (*sullen*) I thought you didn't like flowers.

Joyce You are in a grumpling.

Lucia (*blurting it out*) I hate you . . . I hate your fame, your
glory . . . People coming here to worship – (*Sarcastic.*) at
the altar, to drink of your epiphanies . . .

Joyce (*humorous*) Man shouted at me in the street
yesterday – 'Your books are an abomination.'

Lucia This house is a wake . . . We creep around . . . The
Wake, The Wake, The Wake . . . You are married to it.

Joyce Sometimes I cannot write a single word . . . I have
been in there for hours, the Phoenix Park in Dublin with
three egregious ruffians.

Lucia (*undeterred*) Beckett comes and gazes, crosses his legs
and smokes cigarettes the way you do. (*She mimes it.*) He
jilted me.

Joyce Sam says his soul doesn't have as many brides as his
body.

Lucia (*a little mellower*) One evening he came with us to a party for *Ulysses* . . .

It was in a beautiful garden, with tiny lights twinkling in the grass . . . He knelt down and whispered to them . . . And I wished he would have whispered to me like that . . .

Pause.

I hoped to marry him.

Joyce (*consoling*) Your mother and I, we love you.

Lucia She doesn't. She stopped me dancing. Always nagging about the expense . . . Jealous.

Joyce That's not true. She has cared for you . . . She has put up with your tempers. And when I am writing, she stops your haranguing.

Lucia (*mischievous*) I steal her lipstucks.

(*Sulky again.*) You go out every evening to meet your friends, and have big talk – Ibsen's courage, Mama's hats and the wine, my brother runs with the smart crowd, drinking daiquiris, chasing rich divorcees . . .

(*Sad.*) I think of my friends – Kitten, Helene, Blaise, Elise, Katya, Zdenka, Dominique.

(*Quieter.*) Where are they now, alone in garrets or in madhouses . . .

Joyce Is it the dancing? . . . We will find another dancing academy . . . Forget what it costs.

Lucia (*stroppy*) I don't want to dance again. They turn you into a machine. Those instructors demonise you . . . (*Bellowing the instructions.*) 'Reach out!'

'Free the torso!'

'Rotate the legs!'

'Outward, Outward . . .

Free, Free, Free . . .'

Joyce But you were sensational . . .
You were compared to Isadora Duncan.

Lucia (*rounding on him*) You were obsessed with us, me and my friends, watching every twist and twitch of our bodies . . . Leaping leap-year fauns.
You write about us as if we were vassals – rainbow girls . . .
For your titivation.

Joyce (*taken aback*) I put everyone in my books . . . In Dublin, Pola, Trieste, Zurich, Paris, poets and patriots and washerwomen and nymphets. I put the Prince of Wales in a short story, and there was hell to pay. A Dublin publican threatened to sue me because I named his pub. I am the Thief of Baghdad . . .

Joyce then does his Charlie Chaplin 'tramp' imitation but she does not join him in their usual routine.

So you go into my study and read from The Wake.

Lucia (*a little crushed*) Only once . . . or, twice.

Joyce kneels and takes the mirror from her, dries her eyes with his sleeve.

Joyce What is it? Tell Babbo.

Lucia I wasn't good enough . . . I wasn't you.

Joyce is crushed, and recognises his own part in her sense of unworthiness.

Joyce I . . . love you.

Lucia Do you, Father?
Then let me in?

Joyce Where?

Lucia (*encouraged*) Dance is a book too.

Suddenly she takes off her outer jumper, stands up, barefoot, in a pale blue slip, and begins to dance.

She moves around him with a strange suppleness, but without flirtation. She is not Salome, she is not soliciting, but possessed by the spell of the dance itself.

She then takes reckless leaps and Joyce watches, surprised.

Unexpectedly, she speaks single lines of Finnegans Wake, that he has not yet written.

She speaks a line first, and he picks up the next line, and so on, and on . . .

(*In a whisper.*) First she let her hair . . . fall . . . It flussed to her feet . . .

Joyce . . . in winding coils . . .

Lucia . . . Mother naked she sampooed herself . . .

Joyce . . . from crown to sole . . . She greased the groove of . . .

Lucia . . . her little Mary . . . After that she wove a garland of . . .

Joyce . . . meadowgrass and riverflags, bulrush and the . . .

Lucia (*quickly*) . . . fallen griefs of weeping willow . . .

Joyce . . . then she made bracelets . . . and a jetty amulet for necklace of clicking cobbles . . .

Lucia . . . and pattering pebbles and rumbledown rubble of Irish rhinestones and shellmarble bangles . . .

Joyce stops in amazement.

. . . That done . . . A dock of smut to her airy eye . . . and she sent her boudeloire maids to His Affluence . . .

Lucia stops dancing, pulls the jumper around herself, and a scarf over her face, sits shyly, not sure of his reaction.

Joyce You can come in any time . . . My little Druidess.

End of flashback.

Nora (*weary, to Brigitte*) His little Druidess . . . It was downhill after that . . . Raving, raving . . . she climbed onto a balcony in Rue Robiac addressing a crowd – 'A certain Ulysses on the strand of the island of nymph Calypso wrote with his stick on the sands . . . Blattherskite . . . Blattherskite . . . Blatthershite.'

Brigitte *Wahnsinnig.*

Nora Yes. Mad. I brought out the worst violence in her . . . For a mother, that is a death sentence . . . Jim felt it too . . . Felt his own part in the dark romance. In the end, he had to give in; she would have to be put away forever. Miss Weaver, his great patron, found a place that was said to be humane.

SCENE SIX

Film sequence.
    While Nora is speaking, a white sheet (like a sheet on a clothes line) unfolds rapidly down over a glass panel.
    Image of a large, stone, gaunt institution with steps leading up to it. It has a look of gloom.
    Joyce is leading Lucia up the steps, with Lucia resisting.
    Nora is standing at the bottom of the steps, not engaged.
    Lucia bites and bites the leather button on her father's jacket to cling on to him.

Joyce It won't be for long. I promise . . .

    Lucia has succeeded in biting the button off and spits it into her hand.

I will come and see you.

Lucia You won't. Paris is far away.

    A nurse (middle-aged) opens the door and comes down to take Lucia inside.

(*Shouting to her father.*) They call it corporal chastisement . . .
They're BRUTES . . .

> *Door is closed, but 'BRUTES' is heard offstage.*
> *Joyce goes down the steps – Nora and he do not*
> *speak.*
> *Interior. Small bedroom with barred window, single*
> *wrought-iron bed.*
> *Lucia is sitting on the floor trying to bite into the*
> *button but can't.*
> *She kicks on the door and shouts but no one comes.*
> *Lucia stands by the window and looks out (darkness,*
> *if possible).*

(*In a strangely calm voice.*) He on dry land loveliest liveth.

> *She waves at no one.*

> *Interior. Lucia's bedroom. Day.*
> *The nurse is pulling an overall down over her head.*

Nurse (*shouting*) Raise your arms . . . Raise your ARMS.

> *Shot of Lucia in an ill-fitting grey pinafore, her hair*
> *drawn back severely.*

> *Interior. Dining room.*
> *There is a long wooden table.*
> *Lucia is at one end and at the other is a girl called*
> *Justine, hair unkempt, and laughing for no reason.*
> *In front of each of them, a plate of gruel.*
> *Justine eats hers rapidly.*
> *Lucia picks gruel up on her spoon and drops it in*
> *disgust.*

Justine What would you wish for?

Lucia A circus trapeze.

> *Quite suddenly, she smears the gruel all over her face.*
> *Justine hoots with laughter.*
> *Over the laughter, the clang of a bell.*

Nurse hurries in, holds Lucia by the ear and lugs her out.

Nurse You're for the strap, you are.

Interior. Lucia's bedroom.
Lucia lying face down on the bed.

Interior. Laundry room.
Piles of sheets on the floor, also to be mended.
Lucia and Justine are sitting on a stool, mending a sheet, one at either end. They have obviously been talking and formed some kind of friendship.

Lucia My father's name is Ulysses.

Justine howls with laughter.

Justine Mine bred pigs . . . he loved the slaughtering . . . All the sharp knives hanging on the back door of the barn . . . I held the bucket for the blood . . . You should have heard them squealing . . . squealing. He took slugs of Armagnac and went on cutting. (*She stops suddenly, as if remembering, and isn't laughing now.*) A priest took me from the mountain late one night and brought me here.

Lucia What age were you?

Justine stops laughing and stops talking. The memories are too much. She bunches part of the sheet in her hand and puts it to her eyes so as not to be seen crying.
Lucia goes to her and wraps a sheet around her as comfort. They sit together, huddled.

Interior. Long hallway. Dimly lit.
At first Lucia is seen from behind, pacing and counting. We do not hear what she is saying. When she turns to retrace, her voice is clearer and we hear the words 'one-five-six', which continue on until she falls, weary, onto a stool.

Interior. Same hall. Evening.
Lucia is kneeling by the big door on which she places
her hands as in some kind of invocation.

Ulysses seated on the sands of the nymph Calypso wrote
with his augur's rod – HOME. HOME. HOME.

Exterior. Garden. Daytime.
Lucia is sweeping up. She is alone. She sweeps slowly
and listlessly, like a sleepwalker. Some garden debris is
already stacked in little piles.
Suddenly, there is the sound of a bird or birds (it
would be ideal if it were the call of the cuckoo). She stops
sweeping and listens. She throws the broom onto the
ground, leaps over it, then leaps over the other piles. It is
not a dance. It is more like a child's daring, as to how far
she can go unobserved. Leaves scatter about.
Her name is called offstage.

Nurse Fräulein Joyce. Fräulein Joyce.

Nurse and Miss Weaver walk towards her.
Lucia rushes to Miss Weaver to greet her.

Lucia (*almost weeping with joy*) Miss Weaver! . . . Miss
Weaver! . . . How nice of you to come. (*Different
intonation.*) How are my father's eyes?

Miss Weaver It is almost his fiftieth birthday, and a great
celebration is planned . . . Friends and publishers, from all
over the world . . . He wants you there.

Lucia He wants me. He wants me there!

She jumps up and down with joy. Miss Weaver hands her
a new coat for the occasion. Lucia tears off her
institutional smock, wipes her hands in it, and puts the
coat on.
Lucia takes Miss Weaver's hand and together they
walk off as the nurse watches.

Lucia is in boisterous mood. She sings her father's favourite Irish folksong.

(*Singing.*)
'I am a King's daughter
From the town of Cappaquinn
In search of Lord Gregory . . .'

Justine is seen watching from behind a window.

Interior. An apartment in Paris.
An open door in which Joyce is standing awaiting Lucia. He is wearing a blue velvet waistcoat and his precious rings, leaning on his polished cane.

(*Ending the song.*)
'Oh Gregory . . . let me in!'

Joyce drops the cane as Lucia hands him the leather button which she bit off his jacket the day she was committed.
Table with a tray full of gleaming glasses that tinkle.
Sound of talk and music from salon offstage.
Without further ado, Lucia grasps Joyce's hand and draws him into an impromptu hornpipe.
They dance two or three times around the long table. Joyce is showing signs of exhaustion, but keeps it up.
A summoning bell offstage. Joyce breaks off the dance and sits, exhausted.
Nora, in a very smart couture dress enters carrying a cake-plate on which there is an iced cake with a blue ruff around it and one tiny ice-blue candle.
Sound offstage of 'Bon Anniversaire'/'Happy Birthday' being sung loudly, Nora holds the cake for Joyce to see.
In a mere second, Lucia, with prodigal strength, picks a heavy wooden armchair and flings it at Nora, who teeters and then comes crashing to the floor.
Screams above the noise of the music.
Miss Weaver on the telephone to the police, repeating the same things rapidly

Miss Weaver *Oui. Oui. Dépêche-toi. Dépêche-toi.*

Joyce sits with his face in his hands.
   *Offstage we hear on the phonograph, the voice of
Marlene Dietrich – 'Falling in love again . . . Never
wanted to . . . What am I to do?'*
   A gendarme is buckling Lucia into a straitjacket.

Marlene (*voice-over*)
   'Falling in love again
   Never wanted to
   What am I to do?
   I can't help it . . .'

Film stops abruptly.

SCENE SEVEN

Brigitte's kitchen.
   *From the street a woman's voice is heard singing the
Marlene song.*

Woman (*off*)
   'Falling in love again
   Never wanted to
   What am I to do?
   I can't help it . . .'

Nora (*shocked*) It's Lucia . . . She must have died.

Brigitte goes to answer the door.
   *Lucia enters, wearing a man's overcoat, carrying a
rough stick, her long hair tangled with stray ribs of hay
and straw. She is proud of herself for having found them.
Her voice carries in pitch as she recounts her story (be it
true, or invented). She skeeters from the rational to the
more bizarre, at times resorting to Joycean words.*

Lucia Hello, Mother . . . Hello, lady . . .
   This is a very nice house . . . it has no elevator . . .

Nora Lucia . . . How did you get here?

Lucia (*proudly*) Hermes . . . God of Angels and
Messengers . . .

  I upped my shillelagh and walked.

Nora France swarming with military . . .

Lucia No supervision . . . Everybody fleeing for their
lives . . .

  Doctors, nurses, warders all trying to get to the Spanish
border . . . Not mucher Vichy, Vichy afraid of Gestapo.

  (*Complete change of voice.*) I have restored my father's
good name to the people of Ireland.

  They were not *au courant* with his works.

  I wrote to the papers and got good responses.

  My father is going to be crowned the last King of
Ireland.

  There has been no king since Roderick O'Connor,
who was fond of his drop.

  And one night. . .

Nora Shut up, Lucia.

Lucia (*reverting to the perils of her journey*) I walked at
night . . . In near the ditches . . .

  Trees all dewed up. Fields of the dead.

  A man hanging from a tree, his beard shook with icicles.

  They would have to be cut out of him.

Brigitte All by yourself?

Lucia I took up pipe smoking to keep warm.

Nora No one stopped you.

Lucia Yes they did. A German convoy at a border crossing.

  They were off duty, drunk.

  They threw questions at me.

  I answered in German

  Mein Vater hat sein Buch der Nacht verloren.

I said it a few times and they spoke it in English and
laughed –
My father has lost his Book of the Night.
They spoke to each other and laughed,
then one said she is *verrückt*
and they drove off.

Brigitte (*sympathetic*) *Verrückt*. Crazy.

Lucia I took a train to the nearest town.

Nora On what?

Lucia A train ticket from the dead man's pocket . . .
Later that night I came to a town and there were army
vehicles outside a house. The house had a red light.
I rang the bell.
A girl with a sequined bolero stole answered the door.

Nora (*fuming*) A whorehouse.

Lucia Madam needed someone to clean the rooms
and serve the officers drinks.
(*Emphatic.*) I did not engage in sin business
or walk in the darkle.
I served drinks and played Marlene on the phonograph –
Germans on one side of the hall and Vichy on the other.
One man took a liking to me.
(*Flirtatious.*) '*Elsker du mig Kaere?* – Do you love me,
my dearest?'
I trimmed his sideburns . . . I told him my father was very
famous but very ill . . .
He felt sorry for me . . .
And said he would smuggle me out.

Nora (*cutting in*) From La Baule to Zurich, you got here
without any questioning.

Lucia He told the security people I was his *Kinder*.
When we got to Zurich he went to a Bureau to enquire
where Herr Joyce and family were lodging.

Nora She's lying.

Brigitte No she isn't.
We have to report the names of all the people under our roof so they can be traced.

Lucia '*Elsker du mig Kaere?*'
He gave me these.

She takes from her pocket chocolate and nougat and offers them. Both women decline.
Lucia goes to the stove, lifts the top off and stares in with rapture at the flame. She puts the lid of the stove back on, then removes it again and again.

Brigitte (*very gently*) *Bitte* . . . I would rather you did not do that.
It is an old stove and it's moody.

Lucia folds her hands in apology and half-kneels.

Lucia I love fire. Fire is the colour of genius.
My father took me to an opera of Wagner.
And there were rings of fire all around the stage . . .
I miss Wagner, I miss my father.
Mother, when can we go see him?

Nora We have to wait until the hospital allow us.

Lucia sulks.

Brigitte (*upbeat*) Why don't you go and have a little wash and *Aufpeppen*?

Lucia exits. Tense moment with Brigitte and Nora.

(*Tenderly.*) Show her you love her.

Nora I cannot . . .

Brigitte But she's your child.

Nora (*determined*) Jim is my child . . . Jim is my life . . .
I watched over him . . . We were so poor. We were starving . . . Shuttled from one place to another . . .

I learned to roll Turkish cigarettes to keep hunger at bay. If I gave him a stern look, he would put a note under the teapot begging forgiveness . . . I would see him sit there so dejected and trying to write . . . and he would turn to me in tears – 'Guide me, my Saint, my Angel, everything that is true and moving in what I write comes from you . . . Poor Jim, lonely and loony and persecuted . . . Every door shut in his face . . . He couldn't even get his beautiful short stories, *Dubliners*, published. His crook publisher told him that book would never see the light of day. That he had already burned the pages . . . Jim came back into the house and went straight to the piano and played . . .

Zozimus (*sings the Yeats song that Joyce is playing*)
'Who will go drive with Fergus now,
And pierce the deep wood's woven shade,
And dance upon the level shore?
Young man, lift up your russet brow,
And lift your tender eyelids, maid,
And brood on hopes and fear no more.

And no more turn aside and brood
Upon love's bitter mystery;
For Fergus rules the brazen cars,
And rules the shadows of the wood,
And the white breast of the dim sea
And all dishevelled wandering stars.'

He stops singing.

Nora (*emotional*) That night we took the mail boat and said goodbye to Stepmother Eireann forever.

Pause.

Brigitte O Frau Joyce. We have to find a way to help her.

Nora (*aggravated*) How . . . How?

Lucia emerges in a long lilac dressing gown, barefoot, happy, speaking in German.

Lucia *Nur Einen Sommer gönnt, ihr Gewaltigen!*
Und einen Herbst zu reifem Gesange mir.

Brigitte Your German is very good.

Lucia (*to Brigitte*) Because . . . One summer we went to Locarno.
Giorgio picked fights.
Mama had a beau.
She had beautiful, limpid eyes.
I had a beau too . . .
Father had to leave early to see an eye doctor because he might have to have another operation. He looked so frightened . . . Poor Beppo.
(*To her mother.*) Let's go see him now.

Nora Not now.

Lucia Yes, now.

With a swiftness she goes to the phone, picks it up and speaks without dialling.

(*Affected accent.*) Do you remember me?
You don't . . .
I am Isolde of Chapelizod, Lefanunian of elm and stone, the creepered tower, the strawberry beds, the winnerful wonders, winnerful waters of . . .

Nora Put that phone down.

Lucia (*change of tone, angry*) What do you mean? . . . Get me the Matron at once.

Nora (*shouting*) I said put that phone down.

Lucia grasps the big steel scissors and cuts the telephone cords in seconds.
Nora crosses and slaps her hard on the cheek three times.
Lucia with prodigal strength pushes Nora against the wall, then with lightning speed pins her in with the

sewing machine and starts to stab Nora on the neck with the scissors.

Lucia (*stabbing*) What are you going to do with me . . . Where are you sending me . . . Killallholley, Killallholley, Killallholley!

Brigitte tries to pull Lucia back but isn't strong enough. Lucia starts to kick.

Nora (*frantic*) Tie her . . .

Brigitte reaches for bits of cloth. As she starts to tie her, Lucia kicks and fights.

Tie her arms to the back. (*Shouting.*) BACK.

Lucia Killallhoolley . . . Killallhoolley . . .

Lucia fights them fiercely until Brigitte manages to jerk them back and bind her arms with a leather belt and men's braces.
She drags her to the chair and plonks her down.

(*Zanily screaming.*) Harridans . . . Bitches . . . Vampires . . . She-killers . . .

Brigitte manages to tie first one leg then the other to the divided legs of the chair. Lucia sits spread-eagled.
Brigitte pulls back the machine so that Nora can edge her way out.

Brigitte (*to Nora*) Has she cut the vein?

Nora shakes her head, helpless.
Brigitte pats the neck with a towel.

Let's wash it.

Nora and Brigitte go.
Lucia, like a frightened child, stares out at the audience.
Gradually, she starts to speaks lines from Finnegans Wake, *breaking them up as her ravelled memory comes and goes.*

Lucia Since the bouts of . . . Hebear and Hairyman, the cornflowers have been staying at Ballymun . . . (*Struggling for the words.*) the duskrose has choosed out Goatstown's hedges . . . twolips have pressed together them by Sweet Rush . . . the redthorn have Fairygeyed the hayvalleys of Knockmaroon.

Brigitte has entered while Lucia is speaking these lines.

Brigitte You could have killed your mother.

Lucia hangs her head.

You must apologise to her.

Lucia (*in a childish voice*) Dear Mother and Father, I know I am spoilt . . .
You have both been too good to me . . .
Mother, what is your favourite colour?
I will knit you a pair of gloves for your chilblains.

Lucia starts to weep uncontrollably.
Brigitte takes pity on her and unties her.

(*Contrite.*) Are you sending me back?

Brigitte does not answer.
Lucia starts her next speech, very hesitantly, so that Brigitte does not immediately comprehend it.

(*In bursts of revelation.*) They tried it out first on pigs in slaughterhouses . . .
All the pigs died . . . It was dawn . . .
I am brought to the room
Where the spooks go
And you hear screams, at all hours.
It was dawn
Three men came . . .
One put a heavy canvas over me and tied it to the bedpost.
My head stuck out.
I was shouting at them to leave me alone.

Two fitted a steel cap over my skull.
I begged them not to.
Then the machine is turned on.
I start to jump, jumping Jesus.
They won't stop.
Everything going, my mind, my grasp, my name.
They are cooking my brain. I smell it . . .
The volts go judder-juddery and then it stops.
Awful silence.
They go out.
I am blank.
They'd taken everything.
A bowl of gruel was left by the bed.
This was eternity.
When I came to, my head and temples are burning.
It was evening.
I got out of bed . . . crawled.
Big fat moon, grinning.
A girl's voice from under the window – it's Kitten –
'Hurry, hurry, we are invisible.'
I lunged. Flung myself at that window again and again.
That first sound of breaking glass was gleeful.

Shards of glass clattered and then – (*Triumphant.*) a big jagged panel of it came off in my hands. My Shield of Achilles.

Blood on everything – blood-fest.

The brutes came cursing and snarling in different tongues.

They throw me onto a litter,
I was meant to die . . .
Like the pigs . . .
But I didn't.

Joyce is seen downstage, silent and grave.

Brigitte You're here now.

Lucia (*unsure*) Am I?

39

Brigitte does not answer but climbs the ladder stairs to the attic.

She returns with her wedding dress on a hanger. It is pale yellow silk with flecks of small flowers.

She holds it up to Lucia.

It's beautiful.

Brigitte Try it on.

Lucia hugs both her and the dress, then walks towards the corridor that leads to the bathroom mirror.

Lucia exits.

Nora re-enters with a big white bandage around her neck.

Nora Where is she?

Brigitte She's trying on a dress.

Nora Not your wedding dress?

Brigitte Yes.

Nora (*sharp*) Your wedding dress?

Brigitte She has nothing.

Nora She cannot stay under this roof.

Brigitte (*as if praying*) Behold the sparrows of the air: they neither sow nor reap nor gather into barns – yet your heavenly Father feeds them.

Is she not much more valuable than they?

Nora Is this a rebuke?

Pause.

Don't talk to me about sparrows . . . You don't know what love is.

Long pause.

Brigitte I think I do . . . I lost my husband to the mountain . . . he and another Guide were called out, as men from Italian Resistanza were missing on the Eastern side of the Matterhorn . . .

All five of them swept up in an avalanche . . .

The slab avalanches spare no one and nothing – trees, rocks, chamois, deer, ibex, man . . . they were never found . . . He is somewhere up there on the slopes that he loved . . . Alessandro . . . Let her see her father for a few minutes.

Nora It would kill him.

Brigitte Why would it kill him?

Nora Because he cannot cure her.

Brigitte What are you afraid of?

Nora . . . Of losing him.

> *Nora turns away, ashamed of the breach with Brigitte.*
>   *Lucia appears in the wedding dress, her hair neatly brushed, her face aglow with happiness.*

Lucia I am floating . . .

Brigitte *Che bello. Che bello.*

Lucia (*excited*) Look, Mother, I am dancing again.
    Remember Bal Bullier.
    An annual competition in Montparnasse.
    I designed my own costume . . . I was a fish with scales that glittered, and a mermaid's tail.
    You and Father and all of our friends in the front row, clamouring for me.
    Each girl had to perform her solo piece twice.
    My leaps were prodigal.
    Nijinski m'encouragait.
    We had to sit while the judges went offstage to decide.
    The moment they announced the winner there was *tumulte.*

They were pelted.

'L'Irlandais! *Disgrâce, disgrace. Un peu de justice.*'

A reviewer shouted out, my dancing was both 'subtle' and 'barbaric'.

Called me '*Fille prodige, fille prodige. L'Irlandais! L'Irlandais! L'Irlandais!*'

Lucia dances wildly and Brigitte watches in amazement. Nora looks on, fearing another mad episode.

A tall aristocratic lady in black coat, black hat with veiling and a fur enters. She is carrying a large handbag.

This is Martha Fleischmann, for whom Joyce formed an attraction, in Trieste, many years ago.

Brigitte (*apologetic*) Oh Frau Fleischmann, you are welkem. I must have left the door open.

Lucia stops dancing and crosses to Martha.

Lucia (*to Martha*) '*Elsker du mig Kaere?* – Do you love me, my dearest?'

Martha ignores her and goes straight to Nora.

Martha Frau Joyce.

Nora (*tersely*) Yes.

Martha You don't know me but our lives are intertwined.
My name is Martha Fleischmann.
I knew your husband.
We lived in adjoining streets here in Zurich . . .
You were in Universitätstrasse
and I was in Culmannstrasse.

Nora I remember where we lived.

Martha He first saw me at dusk going up the steps to my apartment. He thought I was a pretty little animal.

Lucia She's a whore . . .
A Deutschland whore.

She takes from her bag the letters, which are tied with blue ribbon.

Martha (*ignoring that*) He stood outside my window, gazing up . . .
My shutters were open.
Luckily my lover was away on business . . .
I reminded Herr Joyce of a young girl he had seen in Dublin long ago . . .
Wading out to sea,
with her skirt kilted up.
Later that evening he left a book of his poetry.
His next letter was so moving . . .
(*She reads.*) 'Perhaps I have lived too long. I am thirty-five. It is the age at which Shakespeare conceived his dolorous passion for the Dark Lady. It is the age at which Dante entered the night of his being. Is it possible for one person to have feelings like mine and for the other not to have them at all? I would like to talk to you.'

Nora My husband is recovering in hospital at this moment.

Martha I know!
All Zurich knows . . .
We regard him as our illustrious son . . .
After all, he wrote most of *Ulysses* in this city . . .
I always keep it beside my bed.

Martha now reads unabated, plucking sentences from different piles at random.

(*Melodramatic.*) 'I see you coming towards me,
young, strange, gentle.
I look into your eyes and my eyes tell you
that I am a poor seeker in a desolate world.
For the love of God send me a line.
I am going to take this letter now to your door,
there is an envelope addressed for you reply.
You have suffered much too in these days as I have.

(*Scanning other letters.*) Did you receive the flowers –
Hellebores, the Lenten rose . . .

(*Turning to another page.*) I saw you yesterday.

Your face gave me a sign

that made my heart leap with hope . . .

Perhaps you understand the mystery of your body when
you look at yourself in the mirror, where the wild light in
your eyes comes from the colour of your hair . . . I think
you are good.

(*Turning to another page.*) It seems to me that you are
the sole ray of light which in these last years has pierced the
darkness of my life. Am I mad? . . .'

Nora (*flaming temper*) Yes, mad. I know the exaltations of
my husband's mind. What have you come for?

Martha (*suavely*) My place in history.

Nora What do you intend to do with these letters?

Martha They are my Secret Garden.

Nora You intend to sell them?

Martha I may have to . . .

Even aristocrats are paupers in war-time.

Nora (*wild with rage*) Letters! Letters! I want no more
letters!

*As if in answer to her wail, letters start to fall from the
ceiling and the wings, like falling snow.*

*Lucia picks up two or three and ceremoniously hands
one to Brigitte and one to Martha.*

*During this scene Stanislaus enters dressed as a
postman – postman's jacket and cap with a big canvas
bag, chuckling with relish as incriminating letters are
read aloud.*

Lucia laughs skittishly as she reads part of one aloud.

Lucia 'Is Giorgio my son?'

Stanislaus snatches the letter from her and reads it eagerly.

Stanislaus 'On the nights when you saw another, did he put a hand under your skirt? If I could forget the girl I loved was false to me.'

Brigitte and Nora now realise that these letters must not be read and they go to the stove to burn them, but Stanislaus steps in.

Nora (*fierce, trying to get it back from him*) They are nobody else's business.

Stanislaus Oh yes they are. He is not your private chevalier anymore.

Meanwhile, Lucia and Martha begin to read snatches from different letters, cutting in on each other.

Martha 'I am a poor, impulsive, sinful man.'

Lucia 'Dear Miss Weaver,
You have given me the most generous help. I wish I could feel myself worthy of it, either as a poet or as a human being.'

Stanislaus 'Your reply hurt me and silenced me. Are you with me Nora or are you secretly against me?'

Martha moves downstage, believing she has found a plum.

Martha 'Noretta mia! I send you a little banknote and hope you may be able to buy a pretty frilly pair of drawers with a full loose bottom and wide legs, all frills and lace and ribbons, and heavy with perfume.'

She gives a sarcastic smile and reads one more line from a different missive.

Lucia All men are brutes.

Stanislaus piles letters into his postbag.
  Nora walks downstage defeated and sits on the windowsill. Zozimus and she do not speak.

*As the letters continue to fall, murmurs from the street
begin to be heard, getting louder as voices shout each
other down.*
Semi-darkness.
The figures onstage stand or sit as if frozen in time.
From the wings street voices are heard.
There is a confusion of tongues and opinions.
It is a farcical, illogical babble of voices and discord.

Man I have it on good authority that James Joyce swims
naked in the Seine in France every morning.

Female Tell us more, Deasy.

Male I wouldn't put it past him. They say he only writes
about mattresses and phalluses.

Other Female What's phalluses?

Male O he's a boyo. Turnipy Tim and Turnipy Jim . . .
Didn't he have Tim Finnegan take his trousers down in the
Phoenix Park to test the temperature of the grass . . .

Female Jesus and Mary, what's Ireland coming to . . . ?

Male Now the arcana of Joyce's methodology is beyond
human comprehension . . .

Other Female Ejaculatory smut.

Hoots of laughter.

Male I knew a woman that knew his aunt. When she read
a few pages of *Ulysses* she fainted. Her daughter put it in
a shed.

Other Male Hang the heretic is what I say.

Male Will someone give us a bit of a song.

*A man joined by two others begins in mock elegy – 'O
come back Paddy Riley to Ballyjamesduff . . . O come
home Paddy Riley to me . . .'*

Female He had a bit of humour. His aunt said that a pound of chops would be better value than the three and six spent on *Ulysses*. And guess what? . . . He agreed with her.

More laughter.

Male (*interrupting*) Didn't he put Dublin on the map . . . like Matt Talbot that mortified his flesh and got Ireland off the jar . . . There should be a statue to him . . .

Other Male (*supporting him*) We'll bury him up in Glasnevin beside Daniel O'Connell, the Liberator, and Parnell that had quicklime thrown in his eyes for his sin.

Female (*shrieking*) Over my dead body . . . A cup of scald on youse all.

Male Ireland crucifies its dead men.

Other Female And women.

Arguments and scuffles happen among the crowd.

Male (*commandingly*) I would like to pose a question to the assembled company.

Pause.

Who owns James Joyce? . . . (*Louder.*) Who owns James Joyce?

It is now bellowed throughout – various tones of voice, some supportive, some outraged – and continues as the light grows foggier and the static figures on the stage are silenced.
Sudden darkness.
End of scene.

Hospital ward. It is front stage as was Scene One, with curtain shutting off main stage.

Joyce, semi-conscious, is propped up on a narrow bed, with two machines attached to his right arm. He is wearing dark glasses. With his free hand he is searching the coverlet to find something.

He is talking to himself, veering between raving and lucidity.

Joyce (*reminiscing*) People ask why I never went back to Dublin and my answer is, have I ever left it?

Zozimus enters singing lines of 'Molly Malone'.

Zozimus (*singing*)
  'In Dublin's fair city
  Where the girls are so pretty
  I first laid my eyes on sweet Molly Malone . . .
  And she wheeled her wheel barrow
  Through streets broad and narrow
  Crying, "Cockles and mussels, alive, alive, oh!"'

  'She died of a fever,
  And no one could save her
  And so did her mother and father before.
  Now her ghost wheels her barrow
  Through streets broad and narrow
  Crying "Cockles and mussels, alive alive oh!"'

Joyce Farewell, my friend. Good Barque. Goodbye. Psalmtimes it graws on me to ramble, ramble . . . ramble.

He tries to raise his hand, but it is too weak.
  Zozimus leaves.
  Miss Weaver enters as he exits, and he bows to her.
  Miss Weaver, aged about fifty, in tweed coat, wool gloves and beret. She speaks quietly and is somewhat nervous.

48

She stands by the side of the bed.
Brief pause as Joyce stares at her.

Are you my nurse?

Miss Weaver It's Miss Weaver.

Joyce (*wandering*) I saw Molly Bloom under a sky full of moonlit clouds rushing overhead. 'I'm finished with you,' she said.
   She had just picked up a child's black coffin and flung it after the figure of Leopold Bloom.
   Who are you?

Miss Weaver Miss Harriet Weaver.

Joyce My father loved me.
   He was a vagabond, and a bankrupt
   as am I.
   He is on every page of *Ulysses*.
   He knew all the old-timers,
   the street cries of the urchins and the washer women down by the Liffey . . .
   No one reads Joyce anymore – *Una vera senilità*.

Miss Weaver You are not senile.
   In a recent lecture T. S. Eliot said of *Ulysses*:
   (*She quotes.*) 'I hold this book to be the most important expression
   which the present age has found . . .
   It is a book to which we are all indebted
   and from which none can escape.'

Joyce You did not like *Finnegans Wake*.

Miss Weaver I said you were wasting your genius.

Joyce I sent you a code –
   Dinn: Oriental mixture of din and djinn.
   If he could bad twig her: beat with a twig . . .

Joyce falls back on the pillows, closes his eyes, exhausted from the effort.

Miss Weaver watches as if she would love to stroke his hand, but daren't.

(*Weak voice.*) What day is it . . . ?
  What date . . . ?

Miss Weaver It is January thirteenth.

Joyce Jesus was number thirteen at the Last Supper.

Miss Weaver Don't speak like that, Mr Joyce.

Joyce Have you brought my snuff box?

Miss Weaver I am afraid not.

Joyce My godfather Philip McCann gave it to me
  when I was at Clongowes Wood College.
  (*Moment of clarity.*) You policed my daughter Lucia.

Miss Weaver I had to,
  she kept running away through towns and villages,
  out into the countryside half naked.

Joyce (*frail laugh*) A child of Pan.

Miss Weaver I wanted to help her because she took a
dislike to all her doctors.

Joyce (*with scorn*) Tweedledum and Tweedledee.
  Doctor Jung and Doctor Freud . . . the Shamans of
Zurich and Vienna . . .

*There is a silence and all we hear is the blood trickling
from the tube to Joyce's blood vessels.*

My father asked me to go to him
  When he was dying. He begged.
  It was in Drumcondra Hospital
  I regret that I did not go.
  I was too frightened
  Too afraid to put myself in the hands of my enemies.
  His last words were

'Tell Jim he was born at six in the morning.'
He used to say 'Is Jim pure mad or half mad?'
I was plunged into a prostration of mind and body after
his passing.
(*Brief flash of memory.*) I stopped writing.
He left me his waistcoat and the family crest.
His voice is in my throat . . .
Can you hear it?
(*He sings faintly.*)
'O! The French are on the say
Says the sean-bhean bhocht'
Do you hear his voice?

Miss Weaver (*nervous*) Faintly.

Joyce Are you not my sister Eileen?

Miss Weaver I am Harriet, Harriet Shaw Weaver.

Joyce (*caustic*) You thought you owned my daughter and
me
With your metal lucre.
Perhaps I am a detestable character.
Perhaps you have ruined yourself by supporting me
throughout my life.

Miss Weaver I loved your writing, from the very first
moment
I was moved by the intense instances of your
imagination.

Joyce My head is full of pebbles and rubbish and flotsam.
The task I set myself, was too much.
Why blame me if I ruined myself for my daughter?
She is a fantastic being, she has a sweet nature, she writes
with an abbreviated language of her own . . .
Invading the world of dream . . .
From the cruelty of others, she fell into the abyss.

Miss Weaver Do you forgive me?

Joyce (*wandering*) Darkness is in our souls, is it not? . . .
Our souls' shame – wounded by our sins . . .

Miss Weaver (*very gently*) What can I do to help you?

Joyce (*desolate*) My daughter. My daughter. She will drown me with her eyes, with her hair.
Lank coils of seaweed hair around my heart.

Pause.

Bring her . . .
(*Whispering.*) Spirit her here . . .
Get the horses harnessed.

Miss Weaver (*anxious*) France is swarming with soldiers,
Gestapo everywhere . . .
I had to cycle most of the way here and pass myself off as an interpreter.

Joyce There are back roads . . .
The routes that Dick Turpin's horse rode.

Miss Weaver (*helpless*) It's . . .

Joyce (*cutting in*) Take your glove off . . .

Miss Weaver takes one glove off.
Joyce takes her hand and traces it over his skull with great tenderness.

Fame will come to her
'Twixt A sleep and A wake . . .
Words . . . all there.
Parole . . . Parole . . . Parole . . .
Feel them . . . feel the flickers . . . the locus of lost things . . .
She already knows them . . .
She will retrieve them . . .
She has done so before . . . conjured my words.

Miss Weaver Perhaps you can tell me and I can relay them to her.

Joyce (*urgent*) Non, non . . . Écrit s'evaporant . . .
. . . A presto, A presto . . .

Miss Weaver (*assuaging*) What is the theme, Mr Joyce?

Pause.
Joyce raises himself up, vindicated.

Joyce Love and Death. Liebestod.

Suddenly, the narrow space is filled with the music of
Wagner and the operatic aria of Isolde over Tristan's
dead body.
Joyce has accidentally disconnected the machine,
which topples down.
Joyce and a German soprano, offstage, together sing
the first lines of the love song.

Joyce *and* **German Soprano** (*singing*)
'Mild und leise
Wie er lächelt,
Wie das Auge
Hold er öffnet
Seht ihr's, Freunde?
Seht ihr's nicht?'

A nurse, followed by two male attendants, rushes in.

Nurse (*commanding*) Aus, aus!

One of the men grabs Miss Weaver by the arm and
another throws her belongings out.
Joyce falls back on to the bed.

Joyce (*calling*) Save her. Save her.

The nurse lays Joyce back on the bed, as he gasps for
breath.
The music of the opera continues, rapturous with its
message of love.
End of scene.
Darkness.

Brigitte's kitchen. Stage empty of letters.
  Stanislaus has gone.
  Nora seated in her usual chair, Martha a distance away, sniffing her smelling salts.
  Brigitte hand-sewing with needle and thread.
  Lucia working the foot machine so that it thuds again and again and again. They are all waiting for the phone to ring.

Nora Will someone please stop her doing that?

Nobody moves.
  Miss Weaver enters in coat but without beret or gloves. Sleet on her face. She senses the hostility between the women.
  She shakes hands with Nora.
  Lucia jumps up with delight.

Lucia Miss Weaver! Welcome. *Willkommen.*
  I knew you would come.

She grabs Miss Weaver's coat collar and launches into a garbled memory.

(*Very animated.*) We were in Bray together . . .
  And we LOST each other on the bus.
  I went upstairs to smoke which is how I ended up miles away at the terminus in Arklow.
  (*Laughing.*) Are you afraid of me?

Miss Weaver Not at all.

Lucia Take me to him.

Miss Weaver It is not up to me, Lucia.

Nora (*loudly*) The doctor will send for us.

Lucia It's all I ask . . . one minute . . . half a minute . . . less.

Nora He is forbidden visitors.

Lucia But not me . . . not his Isolde.

Very slowly, Lucia walks towards each one, appealing without the words. They are silent, as if turned to stone. None answers.

I am not mad now.

Pause.
Lucia turns quickly and climbs the rope stairs to the attic. She walks to the very edge.
There is a strange smile on her face as she speaks.

(*Very fast.*) Sea-words, wind-words. All the birds of the air.
They trolled out right bold when they smacked the big kuss of Tristan and Isolde.
My leaves have drifted from me.
All. But one clings still.

Blackout.

Carry me along, Taddy, like you done through the Toy Fair!
I see you bearing down on me now under whitespread wings, like you come from the Arkangels.

She jumps.
Shrieks from the women below.
Miss Weaver and Brigitte rush to catch her.
Lights back up.
They lift Lucia onto the long table.
Brigitte listens for her breath and Miss Weaver feels her pulse.

Brigitte She's breathing. She is breathing.

Nora rises from her chair, goes to the table and, as though performing a rite, lights the tall candle.
She looks down at Lucia. (What is she thinking?)

Miss Weaver (*to Lucia*) I was with your father, just now, at the hospital and it was of you he spoke.

Lucia (*calmly*) He is dead.

Knock on door, which is unlocked. A Young Boy with a Red Cross badge on his overall sleeve enters and speaks directly to Nora.

Young Boy (*handing her a sheet of paper*) I have been sent by the registrar of the hospital to inform you that Herr Joyce passed away at seventeen minutes to the hour.

Nora Did he say anything?

Young Boy No, madam.

Nora Did he ask for anyone?

Young Boy No, madam.

Nora So, in the end, he said nothing?

Young Boy Nothing, madam.

As he exits by the open door, he steps aside to admit two medicos in white outfits with white caps and tiny slivers of ice-blue needles of light from their sleeves.
They tie her in a straitjacket. She does not resist.

Lucia Father, I hope you have not missed your train.

As she is carried out, she does not look at any of the women.
Miss Weaver and Martha follow the medicos.
Brigitte fetches Nora's coat.
As Nora turns to leave, the image on the back screen is a life-size photograph of Joyce: a young man in blue, full of poetic fervour, caught in the dusk of wonder and creativity.
Nora walks towards it and looks at it without touching it.

Brigitte (*tentative*) Would you like me to accompany you to the hospital?

Pause.

Nora I know I am hard . . . I had to be.

Brigitte goes to the drawer for the rings and gives them to Nora.

Yes. Come with me.

Brigitte exits to get her coat.

Oh, Jim . . . I'd choose you again, above all the men of Ireland and Beyond . . . We made our legend . . . And we'll keep to it.

Brigitte returns with her coat.
   They go out together.
   The candle remains burning.

SCENE TEN

Zozimus walks front of stage and sings powerfully.

Zozimus (*singing*)
   'Then Micky Maloney raised his head,
   When a noggin of whiskey flew at him,
   It missed and falling on the bed,
   The liquor scattered over Tim;
   Bedad he revives, see how he rises,
   And Timothy rising from the bed,
   Says, "Whirl your liquor round like blazes,
   Thanam o'n dhoul, do ye think I'm dead?"'

The End.